Igniting the Luminary Spark:

Help Create A New Age of Personal Power, Happiness, and Compassion

Aaran Solh

Contents

Dedication

Dedicated to the luminary within you.
May it shine the everlasting source of love
through your beautiful body and into the world.

Welcome

This book is based on an interview with Aaran Solh that took place in May, 2019 as part of the Evolutionary Empath Summit hosted by The Shift Network and Bevin Niemann who was the interviewer and organizer of the event.

The Evolutionary Empath Summit was an online event where empaths and spiritual seekers discovered how to embrace their spiritual senses and shine their authentic light on the world. All the interviews and talks as well as the downloadable materials are still available online.

At www.AaranSolh.com you can take The Intuition Quiz to find out what Pillar of Intuition you are currently building. You can also download free guided meditations and journaling worksheets at www.aaransolh.com/inner-circle.

What Does it Mean to be a Luminary?

'There is nothing worse than getting enlightened.' That's basically what my teacher told me. He said, 'don't expect it to be interesting, exciting or thrilling.' One moment you're seeking, and the next moment, there you are. The world is as it is. Nothing is different, except that you're not seeking any more.

I told him, 'Okay, yeah, I get it...'

He said, 'No, you don't.'

And I nodded with a confused look on my face.

But I grew into it—his attempted description of enlightenment. I've even had real glimpses—moments of truly experiencing what he was talking about. Everything simply is. Life doesn't stop, but the passing of time does. Not the spinning of the Earth—that doesn't stop—but the passing of time as you're experiencing it right now, stops, and only the present moment exists. But that doesn't mean I don't make plans for dinner with my wife or desire to do good in the world.

What it does mean, is that in those moments, I don't stress out about it. I don't doubt myself or wonder if I'm worthy of having a good dinner or having love in my life. Those questions are irrelevant; there is no deserving and non-deserving. The very question is absurd. The very idea that I should take anything personally is also absurd. And the idea that something could extinguish my inner light is nonexistent.

In these moments, there is only the satisfaction of understanding life as it is. The great tragedy and comedy of it all. From that understanding, peace, compassion, kindness, and infinite patience arise naturally and effortlessly. And when there's a practical question of what to do, there is only one answer that presents itself. Instead of a confusing barrage of endless possibilities, the answer comes from the eternal voice of truth and wisdom we all have access to—The Invisible Sun within. This clarity and service to the inner light is what is meant by *Being A Luminary*. You become a beacon and lighthouse, shining the light of The Great Intelligence of The Universe (or the God of your understanding) through your body.

Discovering the truth of who you are and being a luminary is a deeply personal and subjective journey. It's intimate. As the ancient poet Rumi puts it, 'When you look for God, God is in the look of your eyes. In the thought of looking. Nearer to you than yourself.' Truly contemplate that for a moment. Not with the mind, but with the body—tune into the non-verbal meaning of it if you can. What is the feeling of it in your body? Allow that true mystery to inform you. To be in relationship with you.

Truly, right now, take a moment to contemplate that.

The Marriage of Solar and Lunar Consciousness—the Ego and the Divine Self.

In this short phrase by Rumi, you can sense the infinite intimacy that the journey to the Divine represents. The stillness pointed to by Rumi and by the teacher I mentioned above, is a type of perfect inner balance that we all seek. In both the Western and Eastern mystical traditions this journey to balance is described as the internal marriage of our lunar and solar archetypes. The solar principle is the masculine, the projective, the active; called *yang* in Chinese philosophy. The lunar is the feminine, the receptive, the passive; called yin in Chinese philosophy. Falling too deeply into either one of these principles, creates imbalance. The masculine imbalance is obvious and is extremely visible in the world today where competition, war and selfishness are all too prevalent. The feminine imbalance is the opposite and leads to stagnation, submission, and internalized resentment. An imbalance of either one leads to conflict and struggles for power.

Being a luminary is about a marriage of the two. The ego (the identity or *small self*) *in relationship* with the *Divine self*—the *lunar* in relationship to the *solar*. One doesn't need to kill the other in order to attain wisdom. One doesn't need to kill the other in order to accomplish tremendous worldly feats and innovations. We must embrace a balance. We can't reject our own solar nature because its imbalance has caused destruction. We can't neglect the need to be receptive and listen to the movement of nature and the stars in order to attain the silence within because for some people this has meant a life of flightiness, endless deliberation, and inaction.

The marriage of the two is crucial to the survival of this planet. We've already driven endless species of wildlife to extinction. We've already destroyed our natural environments to the point where that destruction may destroy us in turn. But with the resurgence of many feminine, heart-centered, spiritualities, this marriage is more attainable than ever. Even the major 'masculine' religions of the world are finding this balance by embracing tolerance and mutuality rather than fighting and destroying the other in the name of God. There is hope. And the best way to support this hope is for each one of us to find this balanced marriage within and become a luminary in their own life.

Never Prepare for Anything

This short book is based on an interview. When I was invited to give it, I wasn't sure what would happen or what words would come through me, so I meditated on it and I prepared. What questions might come? What would I answer? I rehearsed in my mind and there were moments when I thought I said something brilliantly and was bummed I hadn't waited to say it live. I knew that it would never come back to me in the same shape and form.

If you've ever created or written something, you know what I mean. You have an idea and you frame it perfectly in your mind, but when the time comes to write it, say it or build it, it somehow comes out differently. So to truly prepare, I let go and I took my cues from another teacher of mine. She never prepared for anything. All she ever did was show up and be her luminary self. When somebody asked a question, she'd answer, and the answer would be perfect in that moment for that person because she was present and she saw the truth of who the person was and what they were going through.

I stopped preparing. I let go and knew that no preparation could possibly express the wisdom that I could represent if I simply showed up live, vulnerable, and spoke the truth from my heart with passion, love and devotion to the higher self. After all, it was important to me to model what I was talking about! In the interview itself, I felt a powerful flow and did my best to stay connected to the truth even if what I had to say wasn't perfectly articulated or seemed '*too*' bold a statement.

When I received the recording of the audio, I loved what I heard so I had it transcribed and went in to edit it. That proved a bit harder to do than I thought and I almost gave up on it. The way a person talks and the way something should be conveyed in writing are very different. But I did it. I not only did it, I believe I've improved upon the original talk significantly. I clarified concepts and I added material I know will be beneficial to you, the empath or the spiritual practitioner, seeking awakening and true service to the world. I chose to leave the original Q&A structure because I found that even though the material has been reorganized and elaborated upon, that it creates a nice flow and even makes it more fun to read.

I am still learning. Even though I understand that the very concept of learning is ironic. Really, it is all about unlearning. Getting rid of the hindrances and mental/emotional conditioned reactions deeply embedded in my mind. But the work of spiritual growth isn't that of pulling out these weeds. Rather, the work is to shine the light of The Invisible Sun within on my mental garden. Destructive thoughts and other lies can't survive that. And once the weeds are gone, my silent, ego/lunar self can shine more brightly in the world.

My hope is that through these and my other writings you find the peace, freedom and connection you are looking for. That you learn to shine the light from within rather than endlessly vacillate, trying to decide which thought is true and which isn't; or which thought is 'mine' and which thought belongs to 'another' (hint: neither one is true). In the present moment, there's none of that. When you allow the light of the Invisible Sun within you to ignite the luminary spark, there are no questions. This is what my teacher was pointing to. That when you surrender, one moment there's confusion, and the next, there's a simple, non-verbal awareness that radiates outward. How to continuously be and anchor into that non-verbal awareness is what I elaborate on in the pages to follow.

Blessings to you on this journey and may your luminescence always be a blessing to all you know and all who cross your path. May you shine your Inner Sun brilliantly. May it radiate through the love of your beautiful, lunar, and sentient body. May your Ego find the Divine within and live happily ever after as one, being a luminary for the world!

Aaran Solh, July, 2019
www.AaranSolh.com

Definitions

Empath

A person who is awakening to the oneness of all beings and who has become aware of their ability to apprehend the mental and emotional states of others.

The Lunar Self, The Ego

The receptive, emotive, reflective, and silent side of human nature.

The Invisible Sun, The Solar or Higher Self

The light that makes itself known when you enter the deep and beautiful silence within you.

The Sacred Marriage

When the Lunar Self embraces the Invisible Sun as its source of identity rather than seeking it in external sources

Being A Luminary

Surrendering to the Sacred Marriage and allowing yourself to live an authentic life dedicated to shining the light in the world

Igniting The Luminary Spark

The Interview

Bevin:

Welcome to everyone from whatever corner of our planet you are hailing from today. We're so glad that you're joining us and I'm thrilled to introduce our special guest, Aaran Solh. Aaran began awakening as an empath and intuitive at age 15, which started him on a long journey of spiritual exploration spanning over two decades and four continents. He's the author of Empath to Mystic: The Art of Mastering Your Intuition and Fearlessly Being Yourself and he's the creator of The Intuition Quiz. Aaran currently lives in Vietnam with his wife and daughter, where he enjoys teaching, coaching, eating a lot of fresh fruit, visiting ancient temples, walking through rice fields, and splashing around in the ocean. Welcome, Aaran. It's fantastic to be connecting with you today and to invite our audience to learn more about your work.

Aaran:

Thank you so much, Bevin. I am deeply honored to be here and to support empaths, intuitives, and anybody on a path of spiritual transformation to awaken their heart and to be true luminaries in their own lives. I believe that living authentically from the inner voice and higher self is what truly changes the world for the better. Thank you.

Living in Nature Doesn't Always Mean Living in Harmony

Bevin:

Aaran, when we first communicated and I invited you to be a part of the summit, you mentioned that you recently moved off-grid and that just to get to a place where you had internet access would be a four-hour boat trip followed by several hours riding in the back of a truck with boxes of bananas and coconuts. What led you and your family to decide to go off-grid and how long have you been doing that?

Aaran:

Wow. Yes. I haven't had a chance to update my website with that information. It still says that we live in Vietnam. We've actually moved to a small island nation called Vanuatu, which is somewhere in between New Zealand, Australia, the Solomon Islands, and Fiji to give some context. We're living in a really small, off-grid community with only three other families at the moment. The two elders who founded it are currently living in town, which as you described, requires a four-hour boat ride and a three-hour drive in the back of a truck to get to.

When I mentioned that I would have had to go down there, it was in the context of being able to have fast internet. Fortunately, we've made this work with the satellite internet, which we do have on site. Some people might imagine the off-grid location that I'm living in as little huts in the middle of the woods, but it's actually really well-built and well-funded. Like I said, we have a satellite dish for internet. We also have proper structures that are built to withstand the cyclones that come through here a couple times a year. We have vast gardens with fruit trees, local greens and vegetables. We have a river that runs through the valley, and it's just pristine, ancient and beautiful.

It's tempting to think of a place like this as paradise, but it's actually been a very interesting challenge to live here. As I keep telling my wife though, it's the challenges I *want* to have. It's not the challenges of the city where there's constant driving, huge supermarkets, and terrible lighting everywhere. It's the challenge of community living in a small forest. It's the challenge of doing my wash by hand and nothing ever fully drying because it rains every afternoon. It's the challenge of lighting a fire every day to make morning tea and food. And those are just the obvious challenges. There are somewhat surprising challenges as well, especially around social interaction.

Ironically, here in this small pocket of the world I have more interaction on a daily basis with humans than I ever did living in the city—in my house—where I could go into a separate room and close the door. Here, I only have a studio for me and my family. In the city, I didn't have to go out if I didn't want to but here, even first thing in the morning, I have to interact with other families just to make myself breakfast.

As most people listening to this are sensitive to people's energies, they can understand how difficult that is. One of the things I always recommend to people who are in the process of spiritual awakening, or if they already have an intuitive ability, is to create space for themselves as many times during the day as possible and especially first thing in the morning. It is also important to allow yourself to take time in nature. To be nourished by nature and to develop that connection is one of the primary needs of anybody who wants to connect to the truth within themselves or to awaken as an intuitive or an empath; and really, anybody on a spiritual journey.

Energy is always moving through us, and we're always picking up energy from around us. Those of us who are consciously empathic are aware of this and may get terribly confused by it. When this energy is stagnant, it builds up pressure and creates unconscious resentment, making us moody and on edge. Time alone or time in nature is the time we need to 'take out the mental trash,' as one of my teachers likes to say. Time to allow our inner voice to come back to the surface after being buried by so many voices throughout the day, and even at night, from the dreamtime.

Ironically, here in this small jungle community I've actually had to face some social challenges in asking for space. In creating a way for me to make food without having to have conversations with people first thing in the morning. And then, just really taking my time by the river as needed. It's been no different and possibly even more challenging than the city in that regard.

I am grateful that I didn't have to make the eight-hour trip into town to have this interview and I hope I have described what life here is like.

Bevin:

Well, thank you so much for bringing this forward, and giving us a real vision of what it means to do this work so close to nature. You bring up such a great point—that even if something seems really ideal for many people on a spiritual journey—getting out of the city and being in that kind of a pristine environment—there's still this really deep interaction that's required with other human beings. And learning, even in that space, to hold your boundaries, to understand what it is you need, and to take that downtime for yourself. So I appreciate that you're drawing those parallels between what someone may face in a more urban, modern environment, versus where you are. It's really the same!

Wherever You Go, There You Are—
The Purifying Power of Nature and The Inner Sun

Aaran:

It is really the same! As long as you're with people, you're going to have to learn to deal with people. If you go off and live in a cave, completely on your own in nature, lighting fires from scratch, never going into town for anything, then you might think you're living the ideal spiritual life. And yet, even for the mystics of the past who were able to do that, the students inevitably came seeking them, and they had to learn to contain others and discover what it means to truly love and truly be in unconditional compassion and deep listening to each other—and through that, also for the shadow parts of themselves. You know, those dark and judgmental parts that only being around other people can really make surface.

Here in this intentional community, we have both a spiritual intention *and* the intention of our service work for the world, which is creating ecological zones, safe from logging. I am fortunate to be living with people who are spiritually aware of themselves, and who are aware of what these needs are for each of us, so we do respect each other and give that space as needed. There's just always the challenge of standing up for yourself and stating clearly what it is that you need. Being brave enough to face the possible rejection. And even here (or maybe *especially* here, due to the intense proximity of living), that doesn't always happen without emotional charge. It can get heated.

I'm fortunate to be in a place where people listen even through the emotional charge, though. With people who are truly striving to be luminaries in the world and live from their inner truth. Many people who live in the Western world don't have that. They don't have people around them who will listen to them, respect them, and get through challenges with them. And that is definitely one of the difficulties that we all face in the isolated, mind-oriented lifestyle of the West.

That said, the saying, 'wherever you go, there you are' always applies. And out in nature, even more so, because you can't hide from yourself. Whether you are on or off-grid, whether you live in the city or travel to lots of places around the world and meet people, the final challenge of self-realization and spiritual awakening is to stop and face yourself. To surrender and allow the lunar and solar nature to ignite a spark within you that can never be put out. You can't escape it, so you might as well stop running!

Time alone in nature amplifies this principle and expedites the path to self-realization. One of the reasons people may avoid alone time, however, is that the more time you give to yourself, the more you will come into touch with that which is disturbing within you. These are the painful past experiences and self-destructive patterns that you don't know how to deal with. The mental patterns that are piled on top of the authentic luminary *you*. All the painful experiences you are still angry about, and where you haven't been able to see the other compassionately yet.

I'll get more into letting go and forgiveness later. For now, it is simply important to understand that when you come into contact

deal ~ Baggage

with the present moment and into true alignment with nature and the Divine, it can be difficult to contain because its desire is to cleanse you. Its desire is to purify you and ignite the spark of the Divine within. Allowing that—being *receptive* to that on a regular basis—can be very challenging. To the ego, anyway.

Do We Need to Kill the Ego?

The spiritual path is not about 'killing the ego,' as people sometimes put it. I believe this concept of 'ego-killing' is a misinterpretation of spiritual teachings and causes a lot of suffering and internal conflict. There is nothing to kill inside of us. Not even our so called 'negative' emotions or bad habits. The ego is simply our identity. And identities, as most people will have experienced already, shift and change over a lifetime based on the information they are exposed to. As you open up more and more to your spiritual self, your identity will shift along with that opening. It will shift based on higher wisdom instead of other people's ideas. This is the *lunar* self turning inward to seek the *solar* self instead of reflecting the other lunar selves around it. Instead of being the moon of another moon, becoming the moon to the inner sun.

When the ego shifts, it can feel like a death of the old self and you may experience resistance to that depending on how identified you are with who you are and what you believe. It may also depend on how attached you are to the approval of the people who have formed you (parents, teachers, priests, etc.). It's a complex process. When you resist information that contradicts the ingrained ideas you have about yourself or you don't believe yourself to be worthy of something better, it can be difficult. You find yourself looping through misery as you paddle upstream through impossible whirlpools and waterfalls of emotion repeating, 'no, no, no!' over and over again in your mind. Staying in the comfort of the familiar instead of being open to discovery and to shining your inner light.

The key (to quote The Hitchhikers Guide to the Galaxy) is, 'Don't Panic!' The process of spiritual evolution is a process of dis-illusionment. And I know, most people think of disillusionment as a bad thing, but think about it, is it? Isn't it a good thing to be rid of illusions? Is it hard to face sometimes? Sure. Does it feel like a death of the old sometimes? Sure. Is it a death? No. It's change. But from the perspective of an unbalanced solar or 'masculine' force, it's easy to see how this natural and organic process of change and the disillusionment of self has turned into 'killing the ego' and something our human self might be scared of.

The process of change is part of our natural, lunar and physi-cal nature. Think of the moon changing from full to empty. When you are able to embrace this natural ebb and flow between the fullness of self and the emptiness of self and back again, all the energy you spend resisting it and creating blockages is released. This creates space for the inner, Invisible Sun to shine on our lunar, human nature, and ignite the luminary spark within.

The real key to peaceful transformation and growth is building a bridge—a partnership and marriage—between the ego and the higher self. A relationship where there is mutual respect between the body/identity/ego and the spirit/Invisible Sun within. One needs both forces (yin and yang; solar and lunar) to be balanced in order to bridge the spiritual self into the physical world. Just as one needs both heat and wood to ignite a fire.

Many empaths and spiritual seekers have a kind of ironic im-balance of solar and lunar. We are deeply connected to the lunar, receptive nature, where we reflect what others feel and think and are sensitive to the energy around us. When this awareness of our feminine (lunar) nature is not in balance with the masculine (solar) power, we lose ourselves in others and 'become' the other—we let other people be the light that our lunar (ego nature) reflects. We become a moon reflecting the light of another moon instead of a moon reflecting a sun.

It may be that out of a (well deserved) mistrust of the masculine and solar that we do not turn inward to find it. Problem is, we are told over and over again that we have to be more masculine and 'create better boundaries' in order to alleviate our deep suffering and confusion. What happens is that we then try to mimic an *imbalanced* masculine force because we haven't yet healed our relationship with the solar. So even as we try and create better boundaries, we also unconsciously resist them. Unconsciously, we recognize that simply adding imbalanced masculine force to our imbalanced lunar force is not going to work. Two wrongs don't make a 'right,' as I'm sure your mother told you as often as mine did.

If we create a world where empaths and spiritual practitioners are as externally masculine as those who are infringing on them, we will have done nothing to improve the world. We would simply be perpetuating the same patterns that create violent conflict and those that may create a deeply ingrained sense of rejection within us.

Being The Eye of the Storm

You can start to reconcile the solar imbalance by understanding the difference between *force* and *power*. Using force is an imbalance of the solar. Radiating power from the stillness in the *eye of the storm* is masculinity in balance. Force comes from beliefs about what things 'should' be like. Power comes from deep listening and being courageously true to the voice of silence (turning the attention of the ego/lunar nature inward to find and be a channel for the inner sun).

Think of the world famous spiritual teachers we all admire— The Dalai Lama, Pema Chodron, Thich Nhat Hanh, Eckhart Tolle— each of them has a balanced and still quality that also radiates light into the world without any effort. Their surrendering lunar nature creates space for them to radiate their inner, solar, beauty into the world. They are the eye of the storm. They experience the fullness and emptiness of the lunar self simultaneously, and by doing so, become pure and effort-free luminaries.

When you turn the eyes of the ego inward and start taking your identity-cues from the wisdom within, this is when you ignite the luminary spark. You become the eye of the storm when you drop into the center of the whirlwind while everything (all the energy, thoughts, emotions and experiences) swirls around you (whether you think they originate in 'you' or in 'another').

This place at the center of the storm can seem empty, however, which is why the outside-the-self oriented ego is scared of it. But the eye of the storm is actually more full than anything in the physical universe. In this place at the center, the lunar nature becomes receptive and *married* to the solar nature within. Through the power of observation and receptivity, a union is ignited and you truly start to understand the mystical and unspeakable teachings of ancient masters.

From that place in the center, our authentic solar nature begins effortlessly shining through our beautiful bodies and into the world. And when it shines, it dissipates the whirlwind completely.

So, instead of using an artificial and 'mental' solar nature to try and create so-called boundaries, we need to use it to bolster our courage for the journey inward. To shine our way as we surrender into the depth of our receptive, lunar, ability until we meet ourselves in the place of stillness within.

Speaking for the Silence Within

Ultimately, we are on a constant path of purifying and cycling through all the energy that's around us. If we get into a debate with it, it gets stuck. If we think we have to obey any of it, we get stuck. It's our job to cultivate the stillness and recognize the impersonality and inaccuracy of the thoughts we have and the thoughts others have—to move beyond the personal. To move beyond 'this is my thought' and 'this is your thought.' To really see ourselves as allowing the world to spin around us from the silence within ourselves. This is how I see the path of the luminary or the spiritually awakening individual. We are constant transformers of the world around us. Magnetic centers that allow life's energy to move without getting into conflict with it.

As healers, as empaths, as people who can really understand what it means to be in harmony with nature, it is our job to wake up that silent voice within us. Through that inner silence we can be the transformer, and in a sense, be the immune system of the world. Our task is to move deeper into our lunar, receptive consciousness, so that in that core, we can ignite the solar, projective consciousness and bridge them in harmony.

When there is a struggle between what you mentally think you 'should' do and the truth, you constantly absorb and reflect the thoughts and emotions in the energy fields around you and they get stuck. When you ignite the solar energy within you from a place of stillness, not a place of force, you ignite the luminary spark and start to live a genuine luminary life sourced from the connection to the great mystery within. This light then organically burns away all the negativity and darkness wherever you go. You become the sun that shines equally on everyone!

If you are currently an empath (aware of the energy, thoughts and emotions of others), this means you have a calling. It means The Mystic—The Great Intelligence of the Universe within you—is calling you to be a voice for it in the world. When you listen to it, you become a spiritual seeker on the path of awakening. When the silence within calls by awakening you to the illusions of the world and to the interconnected nature of everything, it means that it is now your job to speak for that silence. It is your job to be a prophet and a visionary for a new Earth—for an age when we can all live together in harmony. To be yet another person who supports the great collective of people who are on that journey together. You can embrace this reality of who you are even if you don't have a complete intellectual understanding of it yet, or can completely grasp and channel it right now. Even then.

Bevin:

What you brought forward is just incredibly beautiful and it reminds me of a quote that I saw from one of your writings, which said, "To become a true mystic you must learn that trying to distinguish between your thoughts and the thoughts of others is an endless, looping and exhausting task. And there's actually no difference." Can you tell us a little bit more about what you meant when you wrote that?

Going Beyond Personal Thought

As empaths and spiritually awakening individuals, we are to some degree aware of the interconnection of all of life. Often, from a place of difficulty at first. From a place that feels like we are constantly invaded by other people and their thoughts, opinions, judgments and actions. When you get into the deeper truth— when you truly embrace the silence of your heart and are able to go deeper (beyond the thoughts and emotions), what you will see is that none of those thoughts and opinions belong to anybody. They pop into existence based on the perception of the moment. Based on the senses that you experience the world with. And if you allow them to (you don't *identify* with them), they'll dissipate into the void after they are experienced.

When you experience the world through your six senses (six if we include *consciousness* as a sense, which is what they teach in Buddhist philosophy), you have a momentary perception of what's happening. When other people have an experience of you, in any given moment, they too have a perception of what's happening. Both *your* perception and *their* perception are based on the past. Their perception is based on what they know and what they believe, and it's the same for you. Your perception is based on what you know and believe. These perceptions arise in a moment, and if you give them a place to flow through the silence that you cultivate within yourself without allowing them to get stuck (without a need to question them, believe them or resist them), then they flow through without harming anybody.

It's very, very important for anybody on a spiritual path or who's awake as an empath, sensitive or intuitive, to really understand that the degree of difficulty they may experience on their ath is only the result of whether or not they allow flow. Flow being their ability to observe, disconnect, and release old ideas and patterns. Flow being an open and fluid mind and a fluid body. As an aside, this is why many spiritualities also involve a physical practice of some kind in addition to service work and meditation. This is also why pretty much all mystical spiritualities also involve fasting of some kind as well. The ancient luminaries knew that for this marriage of body and mind, not only the mind has to be prepared, we also have to clear the body and live a clean and healthy life. If the fluids in our bodies aren't flowing well, how can fluidity of mind take root?

This path we're walking is a path of deep healing, deep presence, and deep connection to each other and to nature. It calls for serious introspection, making bold changes, and embracing a firm commitment to truth. It's a path of deep surrender that simultaneously creates connection both to each other, and to God (however you want to describe the power that is the interconnected web of life we're all part of).

What Is the Difference Between Thought, Feeling, Emotion, and Intuition?

Aaran:

A thought is the result of a perception. It is a limited experience—a snapshot of the world in a single moment from a very singular and limited perspective (yours). So, how does a thought evolve? It is important to understand that before your brain interprets a thought into words, the thought is non-verbal—it is a pure experience. Your six senses share input and compare and contrast that input with your memories.

Together, your senses mix to create a momentary non-verbal experience of the present moment. You can do an experiment right now—be silent for a moment and connect to the non-verbal (lunar/receptive) experience of your senses. Be aware of your perceptions—your sense input—and also aware of the gap between that *experience* and having the *words to describe it*. Simply observe and connect to your surroundings via your sight, hearing, touch, smell, taste and consciousness (you can even keep reading). Become aware of the non-verbal experience component of the moment. After a deep breath, allow yourself to observe how that sensory input gets translated into words—these are your thoughts. You can also observe how your perception of the moment gets compared and contrasted with your memories to create judgments or awaken old emotional baggage.

If you've never practiced something like this, you may not be able to move into complete distance from your thoughts for any length of time but you can probably start to tell when a perception becomes thinking. Perception becomes thinking at the point where you are observing the world and then there's a kind of 'narrowing' of that perception. Something in your mind unconsciously and automatically gives your perceptions definition based on memory. Practice this for a few minutes and you'll start to notice. Take a few breaths and focus on your sensory input. Notice it, and then notice how it narrows as unconscious thoughts are formed.

For example, the wind may be blowing the curtains around. In the moment of non-verbal perception there is simply an awareness of that. Then your interpretation sets in and you think, 'The wind is blowing the curtains, it's beautiful and calm.' Then you compare that to your memory and think, 'When I was a child, my mother brushed the curtains clean every day and one of my favorite childhood memories is watching her clean as the light shone perfectly on her beautiful face.' In your body, your breath opens, your muscles relax, and you feel safe as you have this beautiful memory.

But then you think (again based on memory), 'I've been meaning to clean these curtains. Maybe if I do, I can be as beautiful as my mother was in that moment in time. I'm such a lazy failure and I'm ugly to boot. I can't get anything right.' Your body slumps and breathing shallows. You get depressed and suddenly the curtains (and any curtains you see anywhere) create a depressive momentum that spirals out of control. This kind of out-of-control thinking can take you far away from the present moment and being a luminary. To wake yourself up from it, it is critical to develop awareness of your thoughts vs. your non-verbal experiences. This is especially critical because once your thoughts are in play, they generate emotions and feelings that drive you to act in certain ways.

The verbal thoughts you have along with your memories and your non-verbal perception create an *emotion*, which pushes you to act a certain way via a *feeling*. For example: You *feel* like kissing somebody when the *emotion* of love arises in you due to a *perception* of somebody you like being kind, tender, and vulnerable. Perhaps you unconsciously perceive them as matching an ideal you created as a child of what family is (for better or worse) and you experience the emotion of attraction and you feel like marrying them. This can happen even when your higher intuition tells you not to and that it is the result of an unhealthy belief system.

In general, you can see that emotions mostly fall into two categories—craving and aversion—you either want to push away what you are perceiving or you want it closer to you or to possess it. In the example above, you may perceive kindness and tenderness which leads to the emotion of love, which creates a feeling that drives you to move physically closer and perhaps to hug or kiss someone. On the other hand, you may perceive sudden movement, which unconsciously awakens a past frightening experience. You then may have the emotion of fear and feel like running away. This could be the case even though the sudden movement may have had nothing to do with you or may have even been beneficial, like somebody moving to save a child from falling.

The most confusing moments are when these two feelings are mixed. You might have the emotion of love and feel like kissing somebody while at the same time, a gesture that they make or a way they said something makes you unconsciously scared of them. You might also become unconsciously angry if that person suddenly reminds you of a past abuser or somebody who oppressed you in some way. Even though they are not actually doing it, something they do may unconsciously remind you of it and trigger a feeling of running away while simultaneously wanting to kiss them. These scenarios can be tormenting and can cause a great degree of tension in a relationship. To move past them you must develop a keen awareness of your higher intuition and learn how to tell those intuitions apart from your unconscious thoughts.

It is important to understand that a feeling is not the same as an *intuition*, which comes from a place of higher spiritual connection and awareness of your inner sun. It does not come from thought, perception, and emotion. So even though we often use the same word to describe these two things (we use the word *feeling* to describe both an intuition *and* an actual feeling), they are in fact, very different. An *emotive* feeling is more accurately described as a desire. Even more accurately, as a desire to act a certain way (in psychological terms it's called an *action-tendency*).

This desire is either to move closer to (or to possess) something, or to move away from (or to get rid) of something.

An intuition comes from a one-hundred-percent *non-emotive* place. It is ignited in a moment of connection between your ego and higher self. When the ego asks the higher self for guidance and surrenders to the non-verbal experience of the response. You may experience this moment as something 'descending' from your higher, spiritual self, into your awareness. The intuition is always offered in response to a question or request that you have. It is *not* offered in response to a perception of the senses like an emotion and a feeling are. The intuition, in fact, is most clear, when you move into the eye of the storm, having created distance from your thoughts, emotions, and feelings. The place where you have clear receptivity to the silent and still nature of the higher self. Where the perfect harmony and balance of passive and active, solar and lunar, allows *you* to be perfectly *You*.

When you consider emotion, thought, and feeling in this way you can see how so many people are following these emotions and feelings to their own detriment. You may think of your emotions and feelings as being true, but they are not. They are limited snapshots based on limited perception and memory. This is why it is important to develop true self-awareness and introspection—so you are no longer a slave to these feelings. In my book, Empath to Mystic, I elaborate on the topic quite a bit and talk more about how to tell them apart.

How Do I Reshape My Own Emotions and Perceptions?

Many times, we judge how we feel in a situation and try to change it. But it's impossible to change how we feel in the moment because by the time you perceive your emotion, thought or feeling, it has already happened. The hormones and neurotrans-mitters that chemically create the emotions are already in your blood stream and it may take anywhere from fifteen to forty min-utes for these to naturally subside.

Generally, you can speed up the process of an emotion sub-siding by doing a meditative practice, deep breathing, conscious positive thinking, or other stress reducing practices such as yoga, acupressure, or Emotional Freedom Technique. These activities can generate a more positive emotion and therefore a new feel-ing, but they can't change the old one. That one must be allowed to flow, even if it is/was uncomfortable or inaccurate. If you don't allow it to flow, as with ongoing anxiety cases, it could stay stuck for much longer because you keep looping the same perceptions over and over in your mind or judging yourself for having them.

One complaint I hear often is from people who have thoughts that are spinning out of control. They experience a constant loop-ing of the mind. It is natural on the one hand to have thoughts about your thoughts, but it all comes down to the same process that begins with perception. When your thoughts are looping, you are perceiving your thoughts with your consciousness and reacting to them based on memory. Example, I *perceive* a negative thought about myself and then I judge myself for having it. This produces another negative thought, which I then judge myself for having.

When you think about your thoughts and get lost in them, you may be blocking much needed new input. Input from your body, input from your inner voice or from the voice of spiritual guidance. Essentially, you are not allowing your intuition in— you are not connected to the greater whole through your body. When you are in these moments, you can use this rhyme: 'Out of control? Turn to the greater whole.' It's been a great reminder for me. If your thoughts, however, tell you that you are not worthy of that connection, you may feel trapped. At that point, the key is to dis-identify completely with thought and emotion—practicing being the eye of the storm. If you try and change your thoughts, you'll simply contribute to your sense of failure.

If you're experiencing fear, anxiety or panic, the cure is the same (becoming the eye of the storm) but it can be much more difficult as fear (physiologically) hijacks the attention center of the brain. In my book Empath to Mystic, I elaborate on the process that fear creates and provide practices as well as journaling prompts and action steps to help turn it around.

The gateway to experiencing a connection to the 'greater whole' is through your non-verbal sensory awareness of the moment (the body—the lunar self). You must practice staying in the moment of perception and allowing the thoughts, emotions and feelings to happen on the periphery of your consciousness. Since your emotional experience has already happened via an automated process in your mind, all you can do is be aware of it but choose to act differently based on higher intuition instead of emotion and feeling. When you start to practice this (trusting your intuition over your emotions regularly), it sets the stage for an easier future.

On a subtle level when you start to trust your higher intuition, you train yourself to *perceive* differently so that you don't experience the same emotions time and again. This takes time and training which is why the programs I teach are all long term— because transformation happens more effectively when you take small steps daily rather than take intensive steps intermittently or only when you're in crisis. This latter scenario is akin to binge eating followed by intensive dieting. It's not healthy. Waking up to yourself is a way of life, just as maintaining your health and wellness should be. It's not something you do on vacations or only when difficulty arises. One must train the mind so that when crisis occurs, you are prepared and can remain stable.

Balancing The Personal Experience with Other People's Experiences

Many times (and this is especially true for empaths), we sense a momentary *experience* in others (that combination of perception, memory and consciousness) and we mimic it (adopt it as our own). This kind of 'lunar' mimicry is a very natural process that children use to learn from their environment and develop their identity (ego). Neurologists call these parts of our brain *mirror neurons* and generally speaking, as one grows up, they become less and less active as one develops their identity. This is probably not true for empaths, however, where these neurons may stay active for much longer. If these mimicking perceptions are not balanced out by one's own (personal) perception of the world, they can become detrimental as one constantly lives in other people's experiences.

We may blame others for having strong opinions or for being too into their own experience, but it's also up to us to embrace having a strong experience of our own. This involves truly coming into our bodies and embracing our experiential, non-verbal gifts. This is why body awareness is key for most people who are on a path of growth and why I incorporate this kind of body awareness in addition to thought awareness into the online programs I offer.

Circling back around, the key to full embodiment of self and having spiritual perspective on thoughts and experiences (rather than being trapped in and identifying with them) is awakening to the fullness and oneness of the universe beyond thought. This awareness is crucial because it creates a sense of safety and generates healing of old wounds. It's what allows us to come fully into our bodies and enjoy life. For some people, for the first time ever! There's a reason why many spiritualities call this experience being *born again* or *awakening*. You are being born *into* your body or waking up *inside* it.

Building this relationship with the higher self is what I call the Pillar of Connection, and it is the second Pillar of Intuition. In my book Empath to Mystic, I discuss four Pillars of Intuition: Vision, Connection, Receptivity, and Creativity. All four are needed to establish a flow of self-expression and authenticity in your life. When you build your Pillar of Connection, you learn to receive the nourishment you need from a higher power or your Inner Sun. Establishing this deep connection or *sacred marriage* doesn't happen by striving to be outside yourself or to 'go' somewhere else. The waking up happens when you come *into* yourself (embracing your physical *lunar* nature). It happens when you come into your personal and subjective experience and learn to surrender into the eye of the storm and *receive* the solar self while the storm swirls around you.

When you think of waking up in this way (*in* your body, rather than escaping it), it can be a very liberating perspective—especially for any sensitive people. This is because there is so much joy and pleasure in the body and in being present. Many of us must go through a belief shedding process around pleasure, to be sure, as many religions and cultures shun the enjoyments of the, so called, flesh. But balanced enjoyment of love, food, touch, and the other senses, is actually an important part of spirituality in my world view. The Creative Intelligence of the Universe (or the Divine of your understanding), has made it possible to thoroughly enjoy life. This wasn't done in order to watch you suffer trying *not* to enjoy it. I think that kind of repressive perspective is one of the core problems the world faces at this time.

Creating From the Invisible Sun Within—
So You Don't Sink Like the Titanic

Our whole identity (the whole concept of 'I am this,' and 'I am that'), comes from deeply embedded thought networks which we call belief systems. These are deeply embedded into our brains as young children—as infants, as toddlers, and even in the womb. Some people might even say we come into this life with a certain energy—with a certain karma that our spirit carried even prior to that. Thoughts and mental patterns that have arisen and traveled through eons of lifetimes into this world and into *this* lifetime are intertwined into our bodies through the process of birth and death.

As an aside, I do have a slightly different perspective on karma and reincarnation, and I'll share that later. To stay on point for now, it is super important to be consciously aware of the thoughts and beliefs we carry. Even of the different personalities that we carry—as we all have multiple personalities based on our thought systems, and based on the different people and different places that we interact with. We must continuously cultivate an awareness of those. That's what meditation is for. That's what all the healing practices and modalities are for. That's what breathwork is for. That's what psychoanalysis is for. That's what simply spending time listening to nature is for. It's all about the emptying out of ourselves—what some call *unlearning*.

As you continue through this unlearning, awareness building, and purification process, there is a core perspective to continuously look at. This perspective is to receive support from a place beyond your sense-based awareness for that work. To balance your reactive lunar consciousness by focusing it inward in receptivity to the solar, wisdom-consciousness (rather than outward to the ideas and beliefs of others). It is being in a place of receptivity to your solar nature that is really the key to cracking open your meditation practice, healing work or deep listening to nature. To becoming balanced as a spiritually oriented, grounded human being and to igniting the luminary spark within.

If you're going to take away one thing from this talk, it should be to utilize receptivity to your higher/solar nature, to your inner voice, to The Mystic or to the Divine of your understanding. Receptivity to that as your core practice will take you anywhere you want to go. In my book Empath to Mystic, I explain this quite extensively and provide additional practices to help build, what I call, the Pillar of Receptivity.

When you are receptive, everything can unfold naturally and you can learn to be a transformer—shining the solar light from within. You can learn to be the immune system for wherever you are from a place of impersonality—where it's not personal. Where the only thing personal to you is the subjective experience of your own Divine nature. That's the only thing that we ever have to be aware of—the subjective and unique experience of our Divine nature—the connection that we have with it, and the receptivity that we can have to it. It allows us to live our dream. It allows us to speak the truth when truth needs to be spoken. It gives us strength and it gives us confidence.

It is important to realize that you can't create confidence

through your thinking alone—although many people try to teach that. And while to some degree you can change your thoughts, as one of my teachers likes to say, that's like rearranging the deck-chairs on the Titanic. The Titanic is that thought system. It's the conditioned part of the mind and it's going to sink eventually (this is a good thing). You can rearrange the deckchairs on it or the wall hangings to make it look a little prettier on your way, but ultimately, you have to seek (sink into) the silent place within you. You must make that the core of your practice in order to be fully yourself again.

In the Western Mystery Traditions (the mystical teachings of Christianity and Judaism) that place is called The Invisible Sun. When you make that place your focus, everything becomes clear eventually. If you try and change your thoughts with other thoughts, you cause even more internal conflict, stress, and anxi- *accepting God* ety. It is only when you surrender yourself to the light within you and invite it to transform you that true awakening happens. True freedom takes hold, ironically, when you realize that you need a *partnership* (not an assassination of the ego/identity) with your higher self in order to make any lasting change. *God transeforms "you"*

Being the Immune System of The World and Transforming the World You Live In

Going back to the metaphor of the immune system; some of us do serve that place of purification in the world—of help-ing the body as a whole by taking the poisons onboard and pu-rifying them. Burning them away by shining light on The Invisible Sun. Through our awareness and stillne thoughts to flow and dissipate. By doing this in any e we provide a space for other people to feel more connected to their true nature, more connected to the Divine within them, and more silent, which is inevitably what creates happiness. And as one teacher of mine said, 'happy people don't pick up guns and kill each other'.

By being receptive and allowing The Invisible Sun within to shine through us, we make the light visible. And we create the feeling of being seen—the feeling of safety and calm in the people we meet (without feeling depleted). We create an atmosphere where people naturally feel the ability to move beyond the fear they are carrying. Usually a fear of rejection, where they are constantly trying to prove themselves and constantly trying to fit into a mold.

Eventually, we need to move past all that unconscious learning and conditioning. Past all the artificial moralities that are imposed on so many of us into being our greater, internally married, selves. This is one of the amazing gifts that each empath and person on a spiritual journey can embrace if they choose to. It doesn't mean we'll all be healers. It doesn't mean you'll be an herbalist. It doesn't mean you'll be a spiritual teacher, shaman or guru. It simply means that as you embrace that interconnection, whether you are a CEO of a company that is doing something positive for the world, a painter, a clerk, or a carpenter, you will be doing so from a place of presence, which in and of itself brings good to the world. It means you will be a luminary wherever you are and whatever you do.

What Are Past Lives? What is Reincarnation?

I'll backtrack real quick to talk about past lives and reincarnation and give another perspective on that—a perspective from a place of wholeness. What I'm about to talk about comes from a direct experience I've had, but I've also come across it in teachings that I've read. In a sense, we are all living parallel lives as one being. There is no past or present lifetime. In out-of-time quantum-reality it is all happening simultaneously, even if those lives appear to be in the past or they will be in the future (or they are taking place right now on the other side of the world or in a burrow in the ground).

You can think of all the people on the planet (even of all lives that have ever been or will be) as making up one body. To grasp this, think of your body and how 50 trillion currently living cells (and even the googles more past and future cells) make up *your* body and the story of your life. All the cells in your body are part of one consciousness—*you*. And all lives that are, will be, and ever have been make up one consciousness. You might think of this as the body of God.

When you have a past life memory, you may simply be tuning into another cell in the body. Perhaps that cell somehow influences you in this moment in time even though it lived far in the past. It influences you in the same way as other (currently living) cells influence you more consciously, such as your family and friends. How or why? We may never truly understand that until we achieve a consciousness far beyond our own, but the important thing to understand is that they do influence us and that all places and all moments in time are interconnected.

In past life regression you may connect with those lives from long ago and allow healing by releasing any stuck patterns. This is done in the same way as healing in the present—when we meet the patterning of our parents inside of us and heal from that as well. The important perspective to take away from this is really that we are all interconnected and that a cell (human, plant or animal) on the other side of the world, right now, is actually a cell in the same body as you. We are all in this together and we all need to be healthy and serve our divinely inspired function (be our luminary selves) or we will all die along with this planet.

Bevin:

What I hear you saying is a little different than some of the common knowledge that's out on the Internet. What I hear you saying is it's more about showing up and your presence in the world—your role modeling, versus there being some kind of wrongness when taking on other people's problems, energy, and emotions, which a lot of empaths tend to do. Can you tell us a little bit more about, perhaps, that distinction between the two things?

You Have To Be Somebody Before You Can Be Nobody

Aaran:

Yeah. Thank you. It's very subtle, isn't it? Many people talk about protection, and distinguishing between 'my thoughts' and 'other people's thoughts.' And you know what? That's a really important step that everybody needs to take. And while I'm emphasizing the step of falling into oneness, there's a very important step to take where you do learn to protect your energetic field and have that separation from others. As one saying goes, 'you have to be somebody before you can be nobody.' I'm not sure who originally said that but it's become a popular new-age saying.

It is, actually, very important to learn to have an identity of your own. I don't want to underplay it or say that it's not important. Some people are ready to jump into the subjective reality of the

Divine silence within and allow themselves to merge with their solar nature. Most of us still need to do some more *unlearning* work before that in order to prepare ourselves. We need to shift our personalities and belief systems to be more positive (again, not with our own minds, but in receptivity to our solar nature). Otherwise, we find it hard to allow ourselves to be open to the Divine. We unconsciously think we're unworthy of it.

This shift into positivity has to come from a place of receptivity to the Divine within—receptivity to our own inner voice and solar nature. We have to make a conscious and proactive choice to turn inward and be receptive to the voice of silence within. If we don't, then the changes we make are artificial and they will fall apart—inevitably sinking like the Titanic. Whenever you try and reshape yourself from a strictly mental place, it will be just like any other state of being or attainment that you are told is good by an external source in order to fit into school culture, college culture, corporate culture, etc. It comes from a place of desiring to be accepted and avoiding rejection.

The Difference Between The Artificial Self and Authentic Transformation

Just like any of those artificial structures of personality and ways of being you adopted as a child, you can try and restructure yourself from your intellectual mind (which is really a collection of the voices of others—it is not coming from the Divine within you). You might say to yourself, 'Oh, compassion is a good way to be... I can become something better by being more compassionate. I am now going to attain being compassionate!" It is an endless loop because there's always going to be something better—something to improve if you're trying to change yourself while still coming from a place of polarity.

Lasting change comes from tuning into your inner voice, and learning to be receptive to it. You must partner with it—and from that place, to allow a shift in your identity (ego). You must allow the eternally silent place within you—The Invisible Sun—to determine what is good for you and what is not good for you. Allowing it to burn away all that is false and ignite the luminary spark within you.

You'll want to avoid coming from the artificial place of, 'I believe this might be good, because I read it somewhere... I was told that... I *should* be that.' Any thought or sentence that involves an, 'I should...,' *should* raise a red flag. Ultimately, for every person in the world, what's good for them is only going to come from the inner voice. Cultivating silence and receptivity allows that voice of wisdom to awaken from within, and from there, you can allow the restructuring of yourself to happen. And you can learn to have proper boundaries in a way that's loving and compassionate to other people. Otherwise, you will always fall short of true transformation.

If you try to mentally create change and you repeat to yourself, 'I have to have better boundaries. I have to have better boundaries...' what happens? First, you create internal conflict and disappointment about not being something you think you should be. Frustration then builds up and usually, the boundary setting comes out in a burst of anger and you potentially end up destroying a relationship or labeling other people as narcissists. And I've seen a lot of narcissist labeling in the empath world. And there are, sometimes, true narcissists out there, but most of the time when I see empaths struggling for empowerment and calling other people narcissists, it's because there's a struggle for power with another person who simply experiences the same pain within them and is trying to find love in the world. There is a fight to be free that isn't coming from a place of harmony within and seeing the other person compassionately.

Is There Such A Thing As a Narcissist?
How Do We Forgive Without Feeling Depleted?

In my book, Empath to Mystic, I talk about this—how the origins of the empath and the so called 'narcissist' can be traced back to the same issue of being rejected for their sensitivity as children. Most sensitive children experience a large amount of rejection and are never validated for who they are. I experienced this myself as a child but fortunately I had mentors that helped me overcome the internalized rejection later in life.

In the case of the empath and the narcissist, the narcissist becomes emotionally catatonic as a result of the rejection and can only be aware of themselves from a place of darkness and endless emptiness within (they have a constant need to fill themselves up). To try and get love, they fall into an imbalanced masculine force. When the person who becomes the *unbalanced* empath experiences rejection, they go outside themselves. They leave their own body and mind to try and always be aware of what other people around them are thinking and feeling. They do this in order to protect themselves and in order to avoid rejection. They fall into an unbalanced lunar force.

Ultimately, if you trace back the origins, you're really dealing with two opposites on a spectrum. Both originated as children born with a higher sensitivity and who experienced rejection. The same state of harmony, acceptance and love is needed for both these people in order to move forward in life as their whole selves—to move back into balance.

I have personally been the victim of abusers and what we call narcissists, and to admit it, I still hold anger in me about that. Freeing myself from my internal experience of being a victim is an ongoing process. Freeing myself to see wholeness even through pain is incredibly difficult. And one just can't artificially 'forgive' somebody, it has to happen naturally as consciousness expands and it can take a lot of time.

It's also important to remember that forgiveness is not about condoning other people's actions. It is simply about seeing the humanity of the other person and understanding their story. When you see another person's humanity, compassion *naturally* arises. A kind of removed compassion that creates space and healing *without effort*. What gives me strength is that for me it's about healing the planet as a whole. If I can't transcend my personal pain, how will I ever bring true wholeness to the world and prevent such pain from happening to others again and again? My vision for myself and the world, is my anchor!

Creating a vision for yourself and the world is one of the practices I like to give people. Vision, in fact, is what I call the first Pillar of Intuition. Without a strong and clear vision, it is hard to have the strength and determination to follow the path of spiritual awakening, transcendence, and healing. In my book Empath to Mystic, I dive into the subject quite extensively and provide journaling prompts to help people create a vision for themselves.

Bevin:

So, you're talking about a path of transcendence. A place where even if you have been deeply wounded, as many empaths have in the past by their family of origin or personal relationships, being able to come into this place of wholeness. A place where you understand your own need and you can also see the other's needs. Finding that place of forgiveness and compassion eventually for those other people and understanding their path. Realizing we're on the same path. That everyone's following this progression and journey.

Aaran:

Yes—seeing others from a place of wholeness and understanding their need. Not necessarily being the one to fulfill that need—ultimately each of us has to find it within. Trying to be the source of love for another person is often the mistake empaths make. It's impossible. When we find it within ourselves, we naturally radiate it in a way that is *not depleting*. We radiate it in a way that gives the other person choice about whether or not they receive it and what they do with it. In a way that respects the other person's journey even if they are not ready to see themselves with the love that we can see them with.

When we want other people to be the wholeness that we see in them, it helps them. Complaining to them, however, that they are not living up to it, creates a lot of problems. This often happens when we don't realize that the wholeness we see in the other is the wholeness we are seeking within ourselves. When we stop projecting it and seeking it outside ourselves, we lose the need—we lose the addiction to the other person and we find our freedom. Oftentimes, it's the freedom to leave that person to have their own journey and not tie us down. We can't save people who don't want to be saved. We certainly can't save people by being a floatation device that doesn't have its own buoyancy. Buoyancy that is created by the spaciousness within when we find our self-worth via an infinite connection to the whole; the sacred marriage of lunar and solar.

Bevin:

Thank you. What can our listeners do to continue to strengthen their conviction and connection to their inner voice and become luminaries in the world? You talked about a few things—going into nature and going within. Are there specific practices that have worked really well for you, or other people that you know?

Being An Eternal Student and Then Going As Deep As You Can

The world of practices is as infinite as the mind is infinite. There are so many practices that one can do, and ultimately, all the practices lead us to the same place of releasing the practices and operating from a place of connection to the whole. I'm not going to say 'enlightenment.' That is too lofty, and I'm certainly not enlightened. The most important step is simply to be informed by that wholeness—to be in relationship with it. To recognize that your journey is one of relationship building between your ego or 'human identity' and the eternal wisdom within—your inner voice; the Invisible Sun. It's not one of destroying or 'killing' the ego.

How to do that? It's a matter of exploration and finding what works for you. Think of it as your freshman year in college. And in general, think of life as your freshman year in college. You take an intro course here, and that 101 program there. You're going to see what works for you and what doesn't. After that, when you have some experience and more awareness, that's when you say,

'Oh, you know what? This isn't right for me. It served me to get to where I am, and now I can move on.'

Ultimately, I believe it is wise to find a path to be dedicated to. A path where you can go deeply into one practice or another over many years. If you continuously spread yourself thin, jumping from practice to practice or from system to system, all your work will be surface. But until you find that something that resonates for you, do explore the different practices and paths of growth that exist out there. I've created a fun way for people to sample a variety of practices that also takes them on a gradual journey into balancing the lunar nature and meeting The Invisible Sun within. It is simply called, Igniting the Invisible Sun.

As a general rule, however, whatever path you choose, those things that we've mentioned already are probably the most important. These are time alone and time in nature. These are the most crucial components of being able to enter the silence and maintain a true connection within. That said, I will share some specific practices I find universally potent as well.

Practices to Connect, Strengthen and Awaken Your Power and Divinity

Sometimes, I need to sit by the river for two hours with my thoughts spinning, my head in shambles, and my anger and rage going on and on. 'This person said that, and that person did this...' and it just goes on and on until finally, through prayer and receptivity, something subsides and I'm able to come back to that place of silence. There's no specific amount of time, necessarily, that's good to spend in nature. Or if not in nature, then simply alone. You have to take it as needed. Personally, I like to start my morning with it, take an afternoon break, and then an evening one. If you can find 3 times a day to have 20 minutes of time alone, you've already done a tremendous amount for yourself and for those you love.

Now, I'm a family man and it can be hard when my daughter is jumping on my bed asking for breakfast first thing in the morning. I usually wake up earlier than her because I prioritize my practice and I'm always a happier person and a better father when I do that. As you know if you're a parent, however, I don't always have that opportunity.

So, on those days when life takes over and I don't have time to myself, I do my best to bring my practice to wherever I am and steal time for myself later in the day—never abandoning it altogether. This is something that you learn, like any habit. Again, coming back to wherever you go, there you are. If you learn to be and hold a place of silence, love, and connection, then you can bring that into the places of strife or the places of feeling unbalanced. Even when your kids are jumping on you, your neighbor is knocking at your door, and you have a team meeting in two hours that you need to present your work to.

If you're living in a city, you probably have to get up, get out the door, and be with people all day long and you may not think you have these opportunities for silence. But you do if you prioritize it. Even if it means going for a walk in the parking lot on your lunch break. Even if the earth is asphalt, and the air is polluted, you can still look up at the sun or the clouds. You can contemplate where your food came from. You can tune into the Earth and ask for her support. You can say a prayer. You can tune into the Invisible Sun within and to the non-verbal bliss of interconnection.

One thing that can really help is having a sacred object that you hold in your hand every time you do have time to yourself to walk in nature or do a meditation practice. You carry that object with you all day long in your pocket or on a chain. When feeling unbalanced, all you need do is refer back to that object for a taste of being your true self. I've found that to be a really helpful practice in a busy life—to have an anchor point. It can be an object or it could be an anchor point in your body, as well.

For a long time, in my meditation practice, once I attained a certain degree of silence and peace, I would squeeze my thumb. Essentially, what I was doing is using the mechanism of conditioning in the mind to pair the thumb squeeze with the positive state of mind. If you're not familiar with this concept, conditioning simply means the pairing or association of things in your mind. Usually, conditioning has a negative association but just like any mechanism or tool, we can use it for good or it can rule over us. So I've created a positive condition in my mind, and when I squeeze my thumb, it reminds me of that place of stillness, silence and harmony. I'm doing it right now and I can feel it relaxing the nervous system in my body, making me feel more calm, more centered, and in complete trust. Love is even awakening more in me at the moment because I'm using that trigger (or anchor) point.

It's a great practice. And I have a video that talks more about that on my website. There's a free membership area on my website where people can look at videos and download meditations and journaling worksheets. It's called The Inner Circle. That's where you can find the video that explains this concept fully. I call it The Inner Circle because the point within a circle is symbolic of The Invisible Sun.

In addition to the anchor point practice, there's one more practice that I recommend. It is called the Waterfall Practice. It's a simple visualization. You visualize yourself under a white light waterfall being washed clean. Washed clean... washed clean... You can do this practice anywhere you are. You can do it in the middle of a

'ou can do it in your home in the morning or at night. At
it's especially good for clearing away the day. So, visual-
elf under a white waterfall—a very, very simple practice,
.ofoundly helpful for energy clearing. If you have more
time, you can add to that practice by visualizing yourself in a circle
of protective light before you do the waterfall practice.

There are many ways in which to create this protective light.
If you follow an Earth-based spirituality, you can do some kind of
circle casting, or calling in of the four quarters. If you are a Christian
or part of a monotheistic religion, you can invite the Divine or an
angel to be with you on each side for protection, for love, and for
connection. Follow that with the Waterfall Practice. Receive the
waterfall of light from that place of higher connection and higher
consciousness. This full practice of Circle Casting and Waterfall
Visualization is especially powerful and I recommend doing it as
often as you can throughout the day.

Bevin:

Wonderful. Thank you. As a wrap-up for our conversation today, I wanted to circle back to something you said earlier. You talked about this ability for spiritually awake and empathic people to
give back—to be leaders for our world and to help envision a new
era and a new way of being. What do you think is the best way
for empaths and people on a path of spiritual growth to become
leaders who stand for peace, freedom and interconnection?

Is There a Place For True Mystics in the Western World?

Aaran:

Thank you for that question, Bevin. I do see empaths and people who are on a journey of awakening as leaders who can help

shape a better world more in harmony with nature. This is even if you're just starting to awaken and develop a sensitiv what I call The Mystic—that interconnected web of life.

One of the biggest challenges that modern mystics or empaths face in the Western world is the lack of a designated and respected cultural place. In India, you might become a wondering mystic known as a Sadhu. In Tibet, if you have this gift, you might be entered into a monastery. If you are born into a traditional tribal culture you might become a shaman's apprentice and be recognized for it. But in the West, there's literally no more place for this person. In the religions of the West (whether it's Christianity, Judaism or Islam) there is not really a mainstream place any more for the mystic—a person who is a true bridge for the Divine to enter the physical.

We are creating a new culture, though. One where this mystical part of life is restored and inter-connection is honored. As a conscious person, this can take many forms. It can be healing your own body, being a better parent, being a healer for others, an inspirational artist, being a spokesperson and visionary for nature, for conscious business practices, or for sustainability and natural building... anything really. We all fit in different ways. Whatever you choose to do in life, if you do it from this place of sacred marriage within, you will be a luminary, impacting the world in a positive way. One of my teachers loves to tell a story of how the most enlightened man he ever met was stacking groceries at a small market. What you do in the world, doesn't matter. Who you are when you do it, does!

Whatever you are called to be in the world, wherever you are called to work, if you approach it from that place of sustainability and harmony found within (which is your natural place), you will find growth and you will find your place of service, living a luminary life. Every empath and every spiritually sensitive person will grow into this place eventually, when they commit to going there. It's not without challenges. It's not without difficulties. But there are no better challenges to have. The challenges of developing these traits and becoming a truly empowered leader and spokesperson for that harmony found within. Helping people be happy is the greatest gift you can give the world. Even if it's 'only' your children, or the people you serve at work. Remember, happy people don't pick up guns and kill each other. The attention you give people by being present changes the world!

A truly empowered spiritual practitioner is a voice for Divine harmony in the human body, and in the big body we call Earth, or Gaia. And a great way of receiving support for that is not only by committing to the sacred marriage within, it's also turning to your fellow empaths, spiritually awake community, and mystics.

How to Connect to the Mystics of the Past, Present, and Future

There's another great practice you can do, and I have this available as a free pre-recorded guided meditation on my website as well (in the free Inner Circle membership area). This practice is done by tuning into your collective of empaths and spiritual practitioners energetically. You close your eyes, and you simply invite the energy of your artist's collective. Your artist's collective is made up of the empaths and mystics of the world—past, present and future. You tune into that collective and you offer yourself and your gifts to that collective. After you've offered yourself, you can ask for anything you need back from the collective. And wow, is there energy available there for you! You can do the practice right now if you want.

You can receive so much from tuning into the energy of the people who are on the same wavelength as you and who are engaged in the same challenges as you. You can receive much needed wisdom from that place and you can receive so much energy by simply offering yourself to that collective and feeling yourself as part of something greater than just one person. You can transcend the loneliness and overwhelm that you may feel when you're walking down your city block and you can see that nobody really understands what life is all about. If you do the practice of tuning into the collective regularly, it will give you the courage and connection to become a luminary leader; it will help you become who you were meant to be in this world.

Bevin:

Thank you so much, Aaran. I just did that practice as you were speaking and it was incredibly powerful to feel all of these spiritually awakened and awakening people from all eras of history connecting in together. That's our goal with the Evolutionary Empath Summit—to bring that collective together, to nurture and uplift each other, to strengthen our individual work as well as our collective work.

We so appreciate you being here with us today and we thank everyone in our audience who tuned in to learn more about what it means to be a luminary on our planet, how to step into the Divine within, and how to tune into the collective in order to become leaders for this world. Thank you so much for your time today.

Aaran:

It is my pleasure. I'm so grateful to you for creating this. It has actually been a dream of mine for a while to put together more global activities for this great collective of people and to empower us. So thank you for having me and thank you for creating it.

If you are seeking a deeper path to spiritual awakening, empowerment, and intuition development, order Empath to Mystic: The Art of Mastering Your Intuition and Fearlessly Being Yourself.

Afterword:
How We Abandoned Community Living for the End of an Urban Alleyway and Found Paradise.

For years I idolized community living. Especially community living in nature. And I know there are places in the world where it's done right. Where we ended up living, however, wasn't it. At least we learned what *not* to do. As one teacher of mine put it, 'even when you do things wrong, you can always serve as a bad example!'

Now what was so horrible about this spiritual community in the middle of the jungle that we had to pack up and leave after only a few months of living there? And after having moved everything we owned by plane, truck and boat to get there?

We all crave connection, and we all crave an easier life. One where we have people we trust around us and one where we don't have to do *everything*! Everything being: The cleaning, the cooking, the lawn mowing, the gardening, the vacuuming, the child rearing, the education, the plumbing, the woodworking, the income generating work, and all the little tasks life requires. It is the purpose of community living to create this ease by sharing responsibilities so that one family doesn't have to do it all on their own.

At the community we moved to, none of this happened, however. Life wasn't easier. We didn't really share tasks in a collective way. The founders and the 2 families that had been living there the longest, didn't want to do anything in community. Not the cooking, not the gardening, not even the homeschooling. So there we were, 4 families living in the middle of the jungle, but each still living an isolated suburban lifestyle. I found it ironic and incredibly disappointing. As I stated in the interview, though, sometimes, disappointments lead us to disillusionment as well. And while it may feel bad, it's genuinely liberating (I'll share more about that in a bit).

Well, 'when life gives you lemons, you can at least try and make lemonade,' my wife and I said to ourselves. We tried to improve our situation. When we arrived, we initiated community meals and community meetings. We even facilitated conflict resolution between the families and tried to create long-term plans and to define where this community was headed; what its collective intentions were, and how we all fit in. We tried, along with our counterparts, to come up with a common vision but we failed. It seemed we weren't a good fit for each other after all.

I've done some rash things in my life but this move to the jungle to live with people we had only Skyped with a few times over a bad internet connection had topped them all. But I know better than to stay in a place where I'm not happy and am facing dead ends, so we decided to leave. We're glad we had the experience and we're glad it's over. We're glad to be back in our small town in

Vietnam by the ocean. Sure, there's pollution. Sure, there's urban density. Sure, there's economic pressure. But we found a house at the end of an alley where several other families live. And while we don't share meals and we don't share lawn mowers (not that we have lawns—in this part of the world everybody has fruit and veggie gardens), we share fun.

The kids can run outside freely after school. They play ball together. They play hide and seek. They roam freely in and out of each others homes and do art and play games. And that is what I wanted most for my daughter, because I grew up in a similar environment. Where I grew up, we lived in an apartment complex with courtyards interspersed throughout the buildings; the cars were all parked on the periphery so it was safe to roam around. After school there were always dozens of kids outside playing dodgeball and other childhood games, the names of which probably vary from country to country.

I also grew up without much television. Nobody had more than 2 or 3 channels at the time. Before bed at around 7:30pm, with our bedtime fruit snack, we got to watch a sitcom. Earlier in the day there was nothing to watch but news and educational television. Binge watching, the fear of our neighbors, and the T.V. as babysitter just wasn't part of the culture. It was part of the culture to be active and play.

I wanted this for my daughter more than anything, which is why we've spent so much time traveling around the world seeking it. But on some level, I was also seeking paradise. An ideal life where I always felt loved, cared for, and safe. Traveling so far into the jungle to live in pristine nature allowed me to let go of that. I realized I could be in the most pristine natural surroundings but that I would always have the challenges that come with human connection.

So I surrendered my wounded-soul search for a home to nature and the river. And when that artificial, lack-based need was surrendered, something awoke within me. A warm feeling in my belly. Something was born in me that now allowed me to carry paradise with me wherever I went and to attract more positive situations and positive people into my life. And that's exactly what happened. My seeking ended and all that energy became free, enabling me to make better choices for myself.

So here, at the end of my small beach-town alleyway in Vietnam, I found paradise. Calm and laid-back people to hang out with. A home office, a fruit garden, simple markets, a wellness center to offer my work in, and a proper Internet connection where I can connect with you, my dear reader, who brings so much more meaning to my life than being off-grid and isolated in the jungle ever could. Are there challenges? Sure. Anger, loss, and cruelty? Of course. There is no escaping the shadow, no matter where you go. But being a light in the darkness even if the darkness does not comprehend it is what being a luminary is about, so I keep my sight on the goal—the vision of a greater harmony existing. Even if I have to shake it loose from one person at a time for the rest of my life. That's what I'm going to do.

To stay connected, you can take the 42 day challenge in the next section. You can join the free membership area on my website and download guided meditations, videos and journaling worksheets that will help you clear the clutter in your mind. You can also take the Intuition Quiz or read my full length book and tutorial, Empath to Mystic: The Art of Mastering Your Intuition and Fearlessly Being Yourself.

All my love,

Aaran Solh

Www.AaranSolh.com

P.S. If you enjoyed the book, please help out by leaving an honest review on Amazon. It not only helps me out as a self-published author, but it gives others the information they need to make a good decision about buying. Thank you.

Igniting the Invisible Sun:
A Personal Empowerment Program

In the following section I outline over 35 different practices that fall into various categories (such as self-coaching, mystical connection, and mindfulness). They are categorized by type. I've also put these practices into strategic order to guide you on a journey of transformation. You can get the practices delivered to your inbox one after the other at the timing you choose by enrolling in the program through my website.

Igniting the Invisible Sun is especially designed for the beginner looking to dig a little deeper and get a better understanding of what all this spiritual 'stuff' is about. It is like doing a sampling semester at university. It gives you a taste of self-inquiry, mystical practice, mindfulness, and self-healing practices. At the same time, it is designed to take you on a journey of balancing the lunar nature and turning it inward to receive from The Inner Sun.

Visit my website now to start your exploration

www.AaranSolh.com.

Practices To Support Your Journey

I compiled this list of practices for you to browse and choose from when you feel inspired or have a specific need. The list below is not designed for you to practice in order. In this section, the practices are simply organized by type.

Mindfulness Practices

Mindful walking

The purpose: Mindful walking is a way to both move your body and experience a meditative state.

The Practice: Walk as slowly as you can while looking down and forward (looking a few steps in front of you at the ground). Focus on the experience of walking as much as possible and allow the rest of the world to be on the periphery of your consciousness.

Food Origin Meditation

The purpose: To reflect on your interconnectivity, grow in compassion, increase gratitude and the feeling of awe.

The Practice: Before you eat, contemplate the journey your food has taken.

1. Contemplate the journey from seed to plant to fruit.

2. Think about the farmers and farm workers that worked the field. Consider what their lives are like.

3. Ask yourself what those farmers need in order to do their job (the tools they use for example). Consider where the tools came from and the people who were involved in their production.

4. Think about all the people in *those* people's lives, everything they need on a daily basis to survive, and where it comes from.

5. Next, consider the journey the food took from being picked to arriving on your plate. Consider the packaging, the transport, the refrigeration and where the electric power comes for that. Consider the factory or kitchen workers who may have prepared some of what you are eating.

6. Eat with the knowledge that you are interconnected with all these people.

Mindfulness Gong

The Purpose: To help you <u>stay centered</u> and <u>connected</u> throughout your day.

The Practice: Download a mindfulness app (Insight Timer for example) and set it to an interval that is appropriate for you. Each time it goes off, take a few deep breaths and bring attention to what matters most to you and to your vision/mission in life (look up Stating Your Vision under Self-Coaching Exercises below). Each time you take this mindfulness break, feel that vision taking shape and manifesting. You can also simply allow yourself to be in a timeless space, while taking a few deep breaths.

Can be used in conjunction with the Physical Anchor and/or The Invisible Sun practices below.

Media Free Day

The Purpose: Well, if it's not obvious to you that you'll benefit from a media free day then you *really* need a media free day!

The Practice: Turn everything off including your phone. Yes, including your phone. I realize there are practical issues to deal with, but if you let people know in advance that you're doing this, you shouldn't have any problems. Ideally, spend the day in nature. In general, you may journal or read, but you may choose to completely unplug yourself from any input and output, including writing and seeing other people.

Replace Sugar With Fruit Day

The Purpose: Bringing awareness to food addictions and generally, to bad habits. Learning that you absolutely can make positive change for yourself.

The practice: We all have our favorite candy or salty snack that we know isn't in our best interest to eat. Spend one day replacing this item with fresh fruit. Even if you have to force yourself because your body is unfamiliar with the goodness that fruit brings, do it. You'll want to plan for this—so buy some fresh fruit and some dried fruit and carry it with you all day. When you have the craving for the unhealthy food, eat the fruit no matter what. You may also drink water (not a soda) instead, if it feels right.

Belly To Heart Breathing

The Purpose: Without oxygen our body's cells can't thrive. Not only that, but without proper oxygen flow there is always an underlying stress experience in the body. When you consciously breath, your body recognizes it's getting what it needs and calms itself down.

The Practice: Take 20 long belly to heart inhales, each with a longer exhale. When you breath, inflate the belly and continue to fill your lungs until your upper chest is inflated. Set a gentle alarm and do this practice at least 5 times during your day. Tip: Count your breaths on your fingers or use beads (hold 20 beads in one hand and at the end of each exhale, transfer a bead to the other hand).

Alternate Nostril Breathing

The Purpose: Another way to bring awareness to the breath and oxygenate the body. The difference is that this practice also helps balance the right and left hemispheres of the brain and in general, the polarity of the body.

The Practice: Sit comfortably and for a set period of time (5-7 minutes or so) and do the following: With the middle finger of your right hand close your left nostril, breath in and hold the breath. Then open the left nostril and close off the right nostril with your thumb. Breath out and hold the breath out for a moment. Now close the left nostril again and breath in the right nostril. Repeat. For a deeper practice try holding the breath longer at the end of each inhale or exhale.

Emotion Map

The Purpose: To become more emotionally aware and practice being calm in stressful situations.

The Practice: Draw an emotion map in your body: Draw an outline of the body on a big piece of paper. Use different colors to indicate where each emotion lives. Sit and think about times you've experienced different emotions and then become aware of where you feel them in your body. Where does sadness take root? Where do you feel anger? Where do you feel joy? Where do you feel forgiveness? Next time you feel a negative emotion, become aware of it in your body. Then focus on those areas of your body that are active when feeling positive and allow that positive energy to grow and spread into the negative emotion areas.

Unconditional Gratitude

The Purpose: To be able to feel good in any situation.

The Practice: Sit and contemplate the feeling of gratitude. You can think of things you are grateful for if it helps. Now let go of the need for an object for your gratitude. Even let go of general things such as being grateful for being alive. Let go of all so called 'reasons' to feel grateful and simply focus on the feeling. Once you learn to do this, you can recall this feeling at any time. Especially when in a stressful situation.

Silent Meditation

The Purpose: To gradually clear the mind of its thoughts, fears, and past experiences. To connect with the experience of silent and Divine truth within.

The Practice: Sit silently with your eyes closed. There is really nothing much else to it. You don't need to focus on anything. When thoughts or memories come—explore them. When inspiration comes—follow it. When you make a shopping list in your mind or think of about other practicalities—allow it. Simply sit, and don't interfere. The natural healing ability and silent truth of your Self, will gradually be experienced. If at any point you get stuck in the fear of not remembering what you are thinking about, take a break and write it down. Then return to the practice.

Keep a notebook handy in case you want to write anything down.

Body Awareness

The Purpose: To grow the muscle of observation and stillness and enhance your ability to discern between a feeling and an intuition.

The Practice: Sit silently for a few minutes and then start going through your sense awareness one sense at a time. First, become aware of your eyesight, then your smell, taste, touch and hearing (the order you go through the senses in is not important). Next, become aware of your consciousness—the sense with which you perceive thought. Finally, try and hold an awareness of all of them at the same time. Use stillness and receptivity rather than force to do this.

Self-Coaching Exercises

Stating Your Vision

The purpose: To give you an overall focus and purpose so that you know more clearly what to say yes to and what to say no to. Does it align with your vision? No? Goodbye!

The Practice: Ask yourself what really matters to you—think big here—what do you want for yourself and for the world most of all? Boil it down to one or two sentences at most. If it doesn't come to you straight away, use the Stream of Consciousness Writing exercise first (to be found further into this section) and then boil it down from there.

How Did I Become Me?

The Purpose: To recognize how both the pleasant and unpleasant times in your life have created who you are today.

The Practice: Create a table with 4 columns: Memorable moments, knowledge gained, skills gained, and qualities developed. Fill in at least 5-10 positive moments and then 5-10 negative moments in the first column and then fill in the other columns. When you're done, reflect on who you'd be without these experiences and on what knowledge you'd have or wouldn't have.

Making Things Easy

The Purpose: To help you understand why you want what you want and to make sure that attaining your goals will actually get you what you want.

The Practice: Think of a long term goal or desire you have for your life and write it down. Next, ask yourself why you want it and write that down as well. Continue asking yourself why you want it until you've broken it down into the most minute practical as well as mental/emotional reasons and write them all down. Example: I want my own business. Why? So I can have freedom. Why do I need freedom? So I can spend more time with my family. Why do I want to spend more time with my family? Because it feels like I'm fulfilling my purpose in life when I do. Why do I want to feel like I'm fulfilling my purpose in life? Keep writing in this way until you can't think of any more reasons why.

When you're done writing, ask yourself how you can attain each of those final practical or mental/emotional components or states of mind even without attaining the big initial goal. With this new found knowledge of why you want something, you may find that you need to change the long term goal and simply focus on attaining the reasons for which you want that. You may, on the other hand, find your initial goal completely appropriate.

Stream of Consciousness Writing

The Purpose: To make the unconscious conscious and to allow buried thoughts and motivations into the light. This practice can be used to figure out what you want to do in a specific situation, what kind of work you want to do generally, and can help you clarify things for yourself anywhere you feel stuck.

The Practice: Decide on a topic or a question you have. Next, set a timer for 10-15 minutes and start writing. The only rule is that you may not stop writing at all. Even if you feel stuck about what to write, the rule is that you continue writing even if it's the same thing over and over again until the timer goes off. Finally, read through what you wrote and create bullet points out of your writing in order to discover your unconscious answers.

Possible topics are:

- Brainstorming on a project you have
- Asking, 'what do I enjoy teaching others? (then go and find ways to do that)
- Write about what brings you pleasure, what kind of partner you want, what kind of work, etc.

You can take one of the bullet points you discovered in the first round of writing and do another stream of Consciousness Writing practice with that new prompt.

Sphere of Influence

The Purpose: To empower yourself by focusing on what you _can_ do rather than what you _can't_.

The Practice: Make a table with three columns: Things I can control, things I can influence, things I can't influence or control (right now and probably not in the future either). Fill in at least 10 things in each column. You can make this exercise general or you can make it specific, such as around your romantic relationship or job.

Wheel of Life

The purpose: To bring to light the areas of your life where you are not happy and plan ways to improve them.

The Practice: There are 8 areas of life (in this exercise): Health, friends & family, significant other, personal growth, fun & leisure, home environment, career, money.

1. Make a list of these areas of life or draw a circle with 8 sections (you can also download a template by doing a quick Google Image search).
2. For each area of life, define a number from 1-10 to indicate your satisfaction (don't obsess over this).
3. Choose the most important (or deficient) areas. For each of these areas you will ask yourself, 'How can I bring my satisfaction here up one point?'
4. Write down 2 actions you can take for each area of life
5. On your calendar, indicate to yourself when you are going to take these actions. Keep the actions small and attainable so as not to become overwhelmed. Also, give yourself plenty of time to do them so you don't end up judging yourself.

The Three Things

The Purpose: To bring more joy into your life.

The Practice: Write down at least 3 things you love to do (no matter how crazy). Next, ask yourself how you can do one of these things every day. If you find you can't do the thing itself, ask what you can do to get the same feeling. Write the activities down in your calendar.

Being a Happy Teacher

The Purpose: To understand what your gifts are to the world and to practice happiness wherever you are.

The Practice: Thich Nhat Hanh (a well known Buddhist monk) wrote a book titled, *Happy Teachers Change the World*. Each of us has the potential to be a happy teacher. Make a list of at least 3 things that you naturally teach and are happy to. Then ask yourself how you can be a happy teacher by creating more opportunities to offer the qualities, skills or knowledge to the world. What would it mean to you if you could do that regularly?

You can do this exercise in conjunction with the Stream of Consciousness practice asking 'what do I enjoy teaching?' Also, you can do it in conjunction with the How Did I Become Me exercise.

Collage Your Goals/Desires

The Purpose: To continuously remind yourself of what makes you happy and where you want to get to in life.

The Practice: Collect old magazines or grab some from your local second hand book store. Also get some poster board and glue. Cut out images and words that are meaningful to you and keep alive your belief that what you want in life, is completely attainable. When you're finished, hang your collage in a place where it stands out and you'll see it regularly. On your altar is a good place to keep it if you have one.

Boundary Setting Ceremonies

Letting Go With a Gift

The Purpose: To disconnect from old lovers or relationships that no longer serve you.

The Practice: After sitting silently for a few moments, imagine the person you wish to let go of sitting with you. Imagine that from the center of your chest (your heart chakra), a gift emerges (allow that image of a gift to manifest organically for you). Next, take the gift with your hands and give it to them. Physically move your hands when you do this. Wait until you feel or see the other person take the gift and their energy dissipates.

If you choose, you can wait and see if they too give you a gift from their heart. If they do, you may choose to accept it or not. This is entirely up to you. You must honor yourself and be clear about your choice in this instance.

What to do if they do not take the gift or do not dissipate? In your mind, ask them what they need in order to move on. If you hear something and are able to provide it energetically, do that. If you still cannot let go, try the cord cutting practice listed next.

Cord Cutting

The Purpose: To disconnect energetically from relationships or past entanglements.

The Practice: Stand and take a few deep breaths. Think of a person or situation that you want to disconnect from. Intuitively, envision a cord connecting the two of you. In your mind's eye, try and see where in your body it connects to. Through the cord, send your intention to disconnect and ask that the cord between the two of you release.

If it does not disconnect on its own through mutual energetic consent, imagine a crystal clear sword in your hand and with a swift swinging of the sword (literally do this movement with your hands), slice the cord. Then watch the remaining cord shrivel and fall off of you in the same way an umbilical cord would fall when no longer in use. This practice may need to be repeated again and again before you feel a complete, healthy, separation.

Saying No

The Purpose: To create energetic space around yourself and to practice having a strong boundary.

The Practice: Stand in an area with some room to move around you. Take several deep breaths and if you have time, do a Divine Alignment practice (found in the next section *Meditations for Mystical Connection*). Next, bring your hands to your heart in prayer position and after taking a deep breath shoot your hands forward as if to block somebody from approaching you. Simultaneously, take several steps forward saying 'NO!' at the top of your lungs. Or at least as loud as is appropriate for the environment you are in. Take a step or two back to return to the center and make a 45 degree turn to the right, then do the practice again. Repeat until you return to facing front.

*Can be combined with the Cord Cutting practice or with Circle Casting.

Circle Casting

The Purpose: Creating an energetically clear space around and within you.

The Practice: Stand in a clear area and do a Divine Alignment practice (found in the next section *Meditations for Mystical Connection*). Take a few steps forward and call in Divine support based on whatever tradition you follow. If there is no specific tradition you follow, you can simply call on the Divine Intelligence of the Universe to come forward. Once you've finished calling in the first direction, circle to the right 90 degrees and do the practice again here—calling in support as appropriate to your tradition. Do this in each of the 4 cardinal directions, imagining a white line of light connecting the circle when you complete.

[handwritten margin note: Holy Spirit]

Who You Are

The Purpose: To Understand who you give your power away to.

The Practice: Make a list of people who you allow to tell you who you are or how you should feel. Next to each one, write what it is they usually tell you about who you are or how you should feel. These can be positive or negative. Just bringing awareness to this will give you more power in those and other relationships.

Meditations for Mystical Connection

Warming Your Core

Purpose: To feel strong in your body and be able to stay centered while the whirlwinds of life circle around you.

The Practice: There is a center in your body between the bottom tip of your tail bone and the top tip of your pubic bone. There, in your core, there is an orange ball of heated energy. This is your core power. For this practice, stand up and place one finger on the two locations mentioned above. Feel a line connecting them and inside your body, half way between the tail bone and the pubic bone. Feel or imagine an orange ball of light there. As you feel it, simply be aware of your body, your mind, and observe. Stay with this energy center as long as you can, allowing the world, your thoughts, and your feelings to swirl around without reacting to anything.

Once you have practiced a few times, you can do this practice anywhere simply by bringing your attention to this spot. Even without touching your body.

Make an Altar

The Purpose: An altar is a representation of the sacred—that which you can connect to beyond yourself. Having that reminder wherever you are helps you stay connected to that part of yourself.

The Practice: Your altar doesn't have to be fancy. It can be a corner of your desk, your wall, and your car dashboard (and ideally, all three). Place objects or photos on your altar that remind you of your Divine self and of your mission in life (or of your immediate desires). Whenever you do a meditation or self-inquiry practice do it in front of your altar in order to build the energy of the space.

The Eye of the Storm

The Purpose: To train the muscles of observation and of not taking things personally. If you train well, then when you really need it, you can call on this practice in any moment to prevent yourself from feeling overwhelmed.

The Practice: Sit and breath for a minute or two and then imagine yourself in the center of a huge spiraling storm. In the center is silence—all is well while the storm is on the periphery of your consciousness.

Can be combined with the *Body Awareness Practice*.

Carry A Sacred Object

The Purpose: This object reminds you of a higher state and when you bring your attention to it, it can help take you there.

The Practice: Whenever you do a spiritual practice of any kind, have the object in your hand. This way, you become imprinted and associate the object with that state of mind. Referring back to it throughout your day takes you back to a more centered and grounded place almost immediately.

Physical Anchor Point

The Purpose: As with the sacred object, this anchor point is created in order to remind you of your sacred and balanced self.

The Practice: At the end of every spiritual practice or simply any time you feel really good, you touch yourself the same way. This could be the squeezing of your thumb or a pat on your own back. It's really up to you. Small and unnoticeable gestures work better because they can more easily be used in public and in stressful situations.

Fingers on the Heart Chakra

The Purpose: To bring you back to the essence of your being.

The Practice: Sit silently for a while and focus on the center of your chest—your heart chakra (located at the center point of your chest). Next, bring the fingers in each hand together so that the tips of your fingers are touching each other and place the fingers of both hands on your heart center (as if you are pointing with all your fingers at the center of your chest). Allow the heart energy to awaken and spread through your awareness.

Divine Alignment

The Purpose: To align yourself as a vessel and channel for healing light and your higher self.

The Practice: Sit silently and focus on your breath for a few minutes. Next, imagine you have roots growing out of the base of your body and feet. Watch them as they travel deep into the earth, through water, mud, rock, crystal, and molten rock into the core of the Earth. Next, absorb nutrients from all the places your roots have traveled. Soak the nutrients all the way up into your heart center.

Next, visualize leaves and flowers growing out of your trunk and head as high as you can go. Through the leaves, absorb the nutrients the sun provides. Allow those nutrients to soak into your heart center and mix with the nutrients from the earth. With every breath allow that nutrition to spread through your body and mind.

Talking to an Archetype

The Purpose: To receive Divine guidance and inspiration.

The Practice: Decide what your need is in the moment. It might be strength, insight into a problem, healing, or anything else. Do a little bit of research and find a God or Goddess from any tradition in history that is the God/Goddess of what you need help with. You may also find a saint or other holy person that tradition says can help you.

Find a good image that you like of this deity/person and meditate with it. You can sit with your eyes open and look at the image or have your eyes closed. When you are ready, start a conversation or a Q&A session with them in your mind, asking for advice. Feel free to get as granular as you need with them.

Intuitive Astrology

The Purpose: Using astrology as a focal point for your intuition and to gain insight into a problem.

The Practice: Print out your astrology chart, meditate with it while looking at it and then close your eyes and continue sitting for a while. When you are ready, open your eyes and see which aspect in your chart you are drawn to. Next, Google that aspect and see what insight you gain.

Aum Meditation (Mantra Meditation)

The Purpose: Creating a mystical experience via the use of sound.

The Practice: Aum is said to be the sound that permeates the universe and is the original sound of creation. Chanting the sound for even one minute can give you a beautiful and peaceful feeling. If you like, seek other sounds to chant and try those—find what works for you. Chanting has been proven to physiologically affect the Vagus nerve and initiate a calming response in your body.

Communion Prayer

The purpose: Communion is the allowing of the Divine to enter your body, inform your consciousness and re-ignite your awareness of oneness. A communion practice can realign you with who you really are and help you recognize your own divinity by filling yourself up with it.

The Practice: In your imagination, feel what being in proximity to the Divine feels to you. If you can't find the experience in the present, you can recall an experience of the Divine you've had in the past. Next, allow that feeling or energy to move into your body. Visualize and feel it entering every organ and every cell.

The Invisible Sun

The Purpose: To enter a mystical state of connection and receptivity with The Invisible Sun. The Invisible Sun is the source of all light and spiritual nourishment in the same way the visible sun is the source of physical nourishment.

The Practice: Draw a circle with a point in the center and meditate on this as a representation of The Invisible Sun. Next, focus on your heart chakra (the center of your chest) and visualize the symbol sitting there. Finally, see the symbol entering your body at your heart center. Remain as long as you can with the feeling.

Use the Anchor Point or Sacred Object practices with any of these mystical meditations to give you the ability to carry the end result with you wherever you go.

Purification and Self-Healing Practices

Waterfall Practice

The Purpose: To cleanse your energy and feel grounded, clean, and clear.

The Practice: Imagine a pure white light waterfall pouring over your body and washing you clean from head to toe. This practice can easily be done with other people around, as needed.

You can do this practice together with Circle Casting.

Stand Barefoot on the Earth

The Purpose: Both the spiritualist and the physicists agree that when the human body connects directly with the earth, something harmonious and balancing happens, and a connection to the whole is restored.

The Practice: Find some earth and stick your feet in it! You don't have to go far, a small piece around a tree on the sidewalk will do. So will sand in a plastic container in your apartment. Give it at least 5 minutes. Read a book if you get bored, just don't look at your phone or any other screens. Though if you're absolutely desperate, I give you permission to listen to an inspirational TED talk while you sit with your feet in the sand.

Facial Acupressure

The purpose: Relaxation, healing and deep sleep.

The Practice: Download a facial acupressure point map via a search in Google Images. Using your hands, a little roller, or a soft crystal, massage those points while listening to relaxing music. This is great to do before bed. You'll want to keep a dream journal nearby as you'll most likely have powerful dreams and you may want to record them.

Hand and Foot Reflexology

The Purpose: Similar to the facial points, use this practice for relaxation and sleep. You can use it for healing headaches, belly aches and other symptoms you may have.

The Practice: Download a reflexology map from Google Images and massage your feet or hands. This is great before bed, but also works wonders in the middle of a stressful day. If you have a specific health problem, you can look up specific massage routines for that problem.

The Great Giveaway

The Purpose: To clean out your house of old energy and turn over a new leaf.

The Practice: Literally go through your house with a box (or 10) and fill it with things you don't 100% want right now in your life. If you think it might have a future purpose but don't have anything to do with it now or in the foreseeable future, get rid of it. If you used it in the past, but don't now, let it go. Make your house as lean as you can possibly allow. If you can't bring yourself to give things away, at least put them in a box and stash it.

The Expanding Cylinder

The Purpose: To create energetic space within your field and surrender any past and present negativity.

The Practice: For this practice you may sit or stand.

1. Focus on your root chakra, located at the base of your body (on the perineum muscle between your genitals and your anus) and take a few deep breaths.

2. Shift your focus to your crown chakra and breath deep with your attention there.

3. Start to shift your focus back and forth between your crown and your root as you breath deep. With each inhalation focus on the crown, and with each exhalation focus on the root.

Inhale crown
exhale root

4. As you do this practice, start to visualize a thin bright white light connecting the two points.

5. When your feeling of the string is strong, shift the focus of your attention to your heart center and remain still while breathing deep.

6. With each breath, feel the string expand into a cylinder. It slowly expands and starts to cleanse and push out any negativity from your body-mind and energy field. Continue to

allow it to expand slowly while following your breath. If you hit a point where it's hard to expand it further, you can end your practice there and return to it next time or simply wait patiently until it shifts. If you experience any negative emotion during the exercise, this is normal. You may also experience memories of the past that need to be cleared.

7. When the cylinder expands past the body and contains all of you, sit and continue to observe any negativity or past experiences that need to clear.

8. Call upon a Divine force that you feel a connection with and ask them to fill you, heal you and restore you to your bright authentic nature.

9. If you find yourself in resistance to the clearing, it is usually because you are not willing to forgive yourself or others or you are not willing to let go of something past. If you experience this, ask yourself, 'What am I not allowing myself to experience?'

10. Close with a boundary setting practice of some kind (Circle Casting or Saying No).

Can be done together with the Communion Prayer Practice, Cord Cutting, and/or Letting Go With a Gift. Can also be done in combination with Stream of Consciousness writing on a topic of your choice, which you would include at the end of the practice.

If you're having a hard time and feel internal resistance, a good practice to do with this one is the How Did I Become Me writing exercise. Realizing the gifts you received even from life's negative experiences will ease you into letting go.

I hope your practice is fruitful and spreads the light of The Invisible Sun to all who cross your path.

Visit www.AaranSolh.com to have these practices delivered one by one to your inbox.

Acknowledgements

A huge thanks to Bevin Neiman and the folks at Shift Network for supporting the luminaries of the world. Also a huge thanks to my wife, Aryana Solh and daughter Soffeah for being awesome luminaries and supporting me on my path.

Thanks to the folks who provided feedback on the various evolutions of this writing. Especially My mother, Hana Hoffman and my father who provides ongoing inspiration from the spirit world. Thanks also to Annie Londos, Michelle Ford, Amena Lee Schlaikjer, and Harmony Yendys. Y'all are the best!

About the Author Aaran Solh

IT IS MY MISSION TO HELP YOU HONE YOUR SPIRITUAL GIFTS, FIND YOUR LOVE-ORIENTED PURPOSE, AND FOLLOW YOUR INNER VOICE

Aaran began awakening as an empath and intuitive at age 15. His spontaneous awakening started him on a journey of spiritual exploration that has spanned 26 years and 5 continents. Along the way, Aaran apprenticed with healers, spiritual teachers and shamans from a variety of traditions.

His apprenticeship studies and trainings include: Soul Retrieval, Shamanic Journeying, Conscious Dreaming, Rebirthing Breathwork, Rei-Ki, Cranio-Sacral Therapy, Energy Healing, Aromatherapy, Thai Massage, Psychic Development, Vortex Healing, Deeksha, Guided Meditation Facilitation, Bach Flower Remedies, and a variety of meditation techniques.

Aaran has also attended innumerable workshops, conferences, and retreats with modern spiritual teachers such as Adyashanti,

John Perkins, Sandra Ingerman, Tenzin Wangyal Rinpoche, Gangaji, Brian Weiss, Deepak Chopra, and Pema Chodron. Aaran has also been a student of The Western Mystery Traditions (Kabbalah, Gnosticism and The Egyptian Mysteries) through the initiatory system of The Sodalitas Rosae Crucis & Sodalities Solis Alati since 2002.

In addition to his spiritual studies, Aaran graduated from The Evergreen State College with a Bachelor's Degree with an emphasis in Multicultural Counseling. He also studied Chemical Dependency Counseling and received training in Suicide Prevention and Teen Mentoring.

Aaran is also the author of Empath to Mystic, the creator of the Intuition Quiz, and the The voice of Mastering Intuition: An in-depth online program designed to balance and awaken your third-eye chakra and connect you to the source of your intuition & spiritual guidance.

He currently lives in Vietnam with his wife and daughter where he enjoys teaching, coaching, eating lots of fresh fruit, visiting ancient temples, walking through the rice fields, and splashing around in the ocean.

Private Coaching Information at: www.aaransolh.com/about